Pandas

By Donna K. Grosvenor
With photographs by the Author
Paintings by George Founds

 BOOKS FOR YOUNG EXPLORERS
NATIONAL GEOGRAPHIC SOCIETY

Pandas look like roly-poly, cuddly clowns. Their shiny button eyes peek out from black eye patches. Giant pandas are playful and fun to watch. But there are very few of them.

Giant pandas live in misty, high mountains in China.
Even in summer, the days are cold and rainy, but
the pandas keep warm with their thick coats of fur.

The steep mountains where the giant pandas live are covered with thick bamboo forests and tall evergreen trees.

Bamboo is the panda's favorite food. The giant panda peacefully shares his chilly home with such unusual creatures as the golden snub-nosed monkey and the takin, a large, shaggy beast with horns. The little red panda, a bushy-tailed creature that looks like a raccoon, also lives in those same high mountains.

When pandas are born they are very tiny,
no bigger than a small newborn kitten. In the first weeks,
the mother panda hugs her cub to her breast with a paw
as she walks along on three legs. The cub grows
very fast. By the end of the first year the panda may weigh
70 pounds—about as much as a boy or girl 9 years old.

Pandas love to eat honey. Sometimes they climb trees to rob honey from bee nests. Pandas pull themselves up, paw over paw, clinging to the branches like giant black-and-white caterpillars. Pandas may swallow bees as well as honey. Their throats are protected by a tough lining, so a few bee stings do not hurt them.

People have not seen pandas very often
in the bamboo forests, but they have found
panda nests, trails, and feeding places. Pandas
can move very quietly through the forest. Sometimes
they snort in anger. If they are excited, pandas
make a whining sound. But usually they are not
noisy animals. No one knows how many
giant pandas there are. Probably there are no more
than a few thousand of them in the whole world.
Only a few pandas have been taken from China.
Not long ago the people of China gave
two young pandas as a gift to the United States.

Ling-Ling, a female, and Hsing-Hsing,
a male, whose name is pronounced shing-shing,
soon became friends in their new home.
Each panda was given a cage of its own
in the National Zoo in Washington, D. C.

Ling-Ling finds that a bright plastic ring makes a great toy.

and do somersaults like circus clowns.

Pandas tumble, stand on their heads,

In the zoo there is plenty of time for playing games.

In their mountain home the pandas have little time for play. They are too busy gathering food. A panda eats armfuls of bamboo stalks and tender bamboo leaves in a single day. Pandas also sleep a lot, perhaps as much as 12 to 14 hours a day.

Bamboo is hard to eat, and it takes a lot of it to fill
a hungry panda. Pandas use their front paws to hold
the tall stalks. They munch the tender leaves, and
they can also crunch the hard stems with their strong teeth
and powerful jaws. When pandas chew, their ears wiggle.

Resting against a log, Ling-Ling uses
a thumb-like pad on each front paw to pick up
and hold her food and dish. In the zoo pandas eat apples,
carrots, rice porridge, and grass as well as bamboo.

No one knows very much about how pandas live in the wild.

Grown-up pandas wander the mountain forests all alone.

When they are about 3 years old, pandas are already full-grown.

By then a panda may stand as tall as a man and weigh as much as two men. Even though they look chubby and clumsy, pandas are good climbers with good balance.

Exploring a tub of cool water can be fun on a hot day.

their zoo cages must be air-conditioned to keep them

Since wild pandas live where it is always cold,

comfortable during the hot summer months.

Pandas like to play with balls.
Hsing-Hsing waddles behind a toy
and gets ready to pounce on it. But
a panda pounce can flatten an ordinary ball.
Although they look harmless,
pandas are so powerful that special,
strong toys have to be made for them.

The Chinese word
for panda is *beishung*.
It means white bear.
Pandas look like bears,
and many scientists say
that giant pandas belong
to the bear family.
Still others believe
that pandas belong
to a family all their own
in the animal kingdom.

Shy Hsing-Hsing sits up and plays peek-a-boo with a bamboo shoot. The giant panda is one of the most popular animals in the world, perhaps because he looks like a friendly stuffed toy. But scientists are just beginning to learn about pandas. Scientists will learn a lot just from watching them in zoos. Someday they may be able to study pandas living in the wild. To make sure that these wonderful creatures will be around for people to love and enjoy, China has new laws to protect pandas from hunters.

Prepared by the Special Publications Division of the National Geographic Society
Melvin M. Payne, President; Melville Bell Grosvenor, Editor-in-Chief; Gilbert M. Grosvenor, Editor.